The Ghosts of Port Byron

Eerie Tales From an Erie Town

by

Mary Ann Johnson

Sketches by North Country Artist
John Mahaffy

North Country Books, Inc.
Utica, New York

The Ghosts of Port Byron
Eerie Tales From an Erie Town
by
Mary Ann Johnson

ISBN 978-0-932052-60-5

Library of Congress Cataloging-in-Publication Data

Johnson, Mary Ann, 1923-
    The ghosts of Port Byron.

    1. Ghosts—New York (State)—Port Byron.
2. Folklore—New York (State)—Port Byron. I. Title.
BF1472.U6J64   1987   133.1'09747'68   87-24730
ISBN 978-0-932052-60-5

Published by
North Country Books, Inc.
18 Irving Place
Utica, New York 13501

In Memory of Three Lovable Spirits
"Sam"
"Zuke"
&
"J.J."

Author's Note

This book is NOT dedicated to my children, who have long ago learned to run when I begin "I heard a good story today!"

But to my lovely Siamese cat, Mandy; big, gentle Mandy, with his shining grey fur and clear trusting eyes.

Mandy who curled up and slept confidently by my typewriter no matter how it thundered.

No lock or bolt is proof against ghost invaders;
But Mandy is . . .

m.a.

Acknowledgments

I would like to express my appreciation to my Dad, who started telling me ghost stories many years ago in hopes that one day I would write a book about them; to my husband for his inexhaustible patience and understanding when I sat at my typewriter instead of at the dinner table with him; and to the townspeople for their generous encouragement and for sharing with me these exciting and sometimes terrifying events.

To Bob Peel, a Syracuse newspaper reporter, who helped make this book happen by printing my Halloween stories.

A special "thank you" to the PROBE students at the A. A. Gates Elementary School and their teacher, Ann Kreiling, who never lost interest in ghosts.

To the Cayuga County Historian Office, Auburn, New York, for the use of the old photos, I also extend my appreciation.

And last to my hometown, Port Byron, New York, now celebrating its Sesquicentennial, 1837 - 1987.

Contents

Main Street, Port Byron, New York

Foreword

In this quiet, secluded village, shrouded with huge trees and full of shadows, ringed with brown hills and with an air of enchantment, it is not difficult to believe in witches, ghosts and the supernatural.

This book of ghost stories is based on myths, legends and folk-tales. It is for the reader who likes a good, fantastic story about ghosts and their weird behavior.

How the reader chooses to interpret them is a matter that only the reader can decide. How much to believe is again up to the reader. I can only testify that I have collected these tales of actual events, as true; that is, as truth is possible with messages from the uncanny world.

It was probably inevitable that one day I would write a book about the supernatural, focusing particularly upon the ones in my hometown, Port Byron, New York.

Almost every canal town along the Erie Canal has its peculiar and interesting folklore. According to those who live on the banks of this picturesque canal, the countryside is peopled with native spirits.

Often there is a historical foundation which has been dealt with fancifully and enlarged into miraculous proportions. The reader, besides encountering memorable tales, may find it easy to make something of a probing excursion into the past as well.

Ever since I can remember, listeners have shivered with delight when hearing stories of terrifying events while sitting safely and comfortably in their homes.

Most of the people in the early nineteenth century were isolated from the big cities and lacked modern communications. They looked to the traveling story tellers for their entertainment. Those artists traveled up and down the Erie Canal yearly, stopping by the towns for a day or two. They would take as long as one evening to tell a single story. You could hear these tales all over the country but they would give them local details, have them happen just the next town away. And most people believed every word of it.

I find that ghosts come and go year after year in our town. Some are in residence as I type this page. Have you ever met one? The important thing is not to be afraid if you should happen to see one.

Some of the "old timers" in our town have told me that my dad always saw a ghost whenever he needed five cents for a trip to the candy store. After such an encounter candy helped to calm him down, they believed.

I have been interested in ghosts because my relatives told eerie, terrifying stories about them. A special time for these frightening tales, as I remember, was at a "wake." When friends and relatives watched over the body of a dead person all night, just before burial, it seemed like the appropriate time—when all were feeling a little jittery and afraid of the unknown . . . death.

Evidently at least some occurrences are genuine and reveal to us an aspect of man and the universe that we do not understand.

Of course, I don't believe in ghosts although I am aware that we have no final evidence against them. I am no longer a skeptic, but an agnostic, if that is one who doesn't know what to believe but is keeping an open mind.

In my stories, I have presented only those accounts which seem to be thoroughly substantiated through old family records and the personal experiences of reliable individuals.

I have found that most of the villagers wanted to believe that there was no truth in the stories of the supernatural happenings, but they still shook their heads when ill fortune befell any one of them. In their hearts they knew that an unfriendly spirit was responsible.

Mary Ann (VanDitto) Johnson

A Little Something About Ghosts

Some ghosts make a perishing nuisance of themselves and give people the jitters for no reason whatever. They do jokery tricks such as shoes tumbling about, pictures falling off the walls, pans slipping to the floor, door latches starting to move up and down, something knocking on the underside of the table, and, footsteps going across the rooms, up and down stairs, shaking the house at every step.

There are false ghosts who are actually thought to be devils in disguise. Some ghosts try to reveal where they have hidden a valuable object or money. Ghosts have been known to warn leaders of some approaching danger.

Did you know that all the ghosts and witches of the country are expected to congregate during the winter solstice on the longest night of the year, December 22nd?

Crossroads are noted for their many hair-raising incidents. Hauntings at crossroads are usually thought to be caused by witches probably because they are supposed to have used them for meeting places. There's one spooky spot where ghosts hung out and that was along the Towpath road of the Erie Canal. This crossroad was haunted by two ghosts and several witches.

One ghost was the headless woman dressed in black who terrorized horses making them shy by suddenly jumping out from the darkness and keeping alongside them no matter how hard they galloped. Several drownings were blamed on this ghost.

The other ghost was thought to be an old man, who was murdered on the lock's walkway. He would approach anyone on the towpath with a chilling scream of laughter and then keep pace with the travelers. One story tells of this ghost keeping up with a Model T Ford owned by Furry.

Then there is the "horse and buggy"—another unidentified ghost from the past. There seems to be good evidence that over the years unaccountable noises resembling galloping horses have been heard. Variations of the legend suggested that the ghost was that of Farmer Jim who drowned with his team and buggy in the old Erie.

We have discussed ghosts . . . what about a poltergeist?

This is the name given to the spirit thought to be responsible for a particular kind of disturbance, which is quite different from a haunting, but just as mystifying.

A typical poltergeist case is made up of two basic kinds of events. One, objects seem to move by themselves. They may move in any variety of ways, up or down, fast or slow. The objects may be light or heavy. Occasionally the movements damage something the object strikes. People may even be struck by these flying objects. And two, there are noises, usually in the form of rappings, scrapings, knocks, thumps or other persuasive sounds. Sometimes more like those of haunting footsteps.

A poltergeist disturbance usually goes on in a particular house for a period of just a few days or weeks and then stops either gradually or suddenly. It is thought that a poltergeist occurrence may have something to do with a person living in the house. Often they occur near one particular family member. Aunt Marguerite had such an experience.

There is a theory that a poltergeist obtains its energy from an adolescent. It seems Aunt Marguerite had the most problems with this ghost. One of the first apparently unaccountable incidents concerned the movement of her chair near the bed. Every day she found it moved to the opposite side of the room, and at night it creaked from the weight of the invisible someone who came to lounge after dark.

Several times she had seen objects in flight. One night a mirror fell off the wall. An odd thing about this incident is that the mirror was a heavy one, yet she hardly felt it strike her. It was perhaps a gentle warning of the ghost's presence.

Auntie always had the feeling that there was somebody in the house besides her. She said she had a keen scent for ghosts and could smell one if it was in a room.

These allegedly paranormal happenings took place in her King Street home. My Aunt Marguerite, who was sixteen when the happenings began, is responsible for the clearest and most concise accounts of the bizarre experiences in her neighborhood. She never showed a trace of fear in her story telling.

There are various local stories about a poltergeist named "Kyfast." When the residents on the northside of the Erie became aware of the poltergeist, its manifestations became more frequent. Soon the young children were calling the ghost by name, Kyfast, and chasing it from room to room. It was strange that none of the family members seemed unduly upset by its presence, except the animals who used to crawl away and hide, trembling with fear.

DOORS LOCKED? WINDOWS BARRED?

Time to start reading these ghost stories.

1

The Last Indian: Black Jenny

Near a cloud of morning mist, Black Jenny's canoe glided down the Owasco Outlet. She paddled the little craft through the waves for hours. The moon set, the sun rose and still she paddled. Not until late the next day did she reach her destination. Leaving the canoe tied to a tree trunk on the rocky bank, she began her search for the burial grounds of her people.

The land out there was hilly and from the bank of the outlet it was hard to see what was coming. Some of the birch trees had trunks that divided near the ground and their giant limbs sloped enough so that Jenny could climb them. From the dust in the sky, she could tell whether someone was following her. From a faint trail of hoofprints, a patch of crushed grass, she could interpret the nature and size of the party . . . how long ago it had passed that way, where it had come from and where it was going.

It was the beginning of the spring moon—"the time of hot weather soon." This spring her world was still wild, free and vast! A lone Indian worshipper wrapped in a buffalo robe prayed to the sun and moon idols—made out of animal skin, grass and twigs. Everyone knew it was Black Jenny! Her copper-skinned face, wrinkled from long years beneath the sun, was serious, thoughtful and deliberate.

It is believed that Jenny's tribe arrived first on the west bank of the Seneca River. At a time faded from memory, her people had come into this land as conquerors. Now she alone remained and the vast territory was divided among a loose-knit confederation of whites that mostly went their separate ways and sometimes even warred on one another.

During the war years, a number of Indians chose to join the whites rather than fight them. A variation of this story tells of the great Iroquois league breaking up and retreating from the eastern lands to the mountains. It was rumored that Black Jenny hid in the deep forest with the Cayugas for awhile where the soldiers could not find her. The army had authorization to clear away, by what-ever means, all the Indians who lingered outside the boundaries the white men had set. All of this was long ago; nevertheless, Black Jenny remained bitterly angry. Her people had been forced, by white pressure, out of the regions that carried their names.

White settlements sprang up along the outlet . . . towns grew . . . and still Jenny stayed on in Port Byron. She was pursuing a friendship with the whites with her small laundry service. She must have entered the village with conflicting emotions because no genuine attempts had been made to ease her into the society of whites.

In the dirt track that formed the village street stood a wooden wagon harnessed to a shabby pony and driven by Jenny. (The first roads through the town followed quite closely the Indian trails and she knew them all.) Twice a day, she picked up the dirty clothes from the settlers in town and returned them cleaned and pressed, often on the same day. This was her only means of income.

Jenny would never speak when a favor was shown her. She told one of her customers at the Sarony Boarding House that when kindness is shown to an Indian, he feels it in his heart and the heart has no tongue.

For most of her life, she lived in a one-room, unpainted hut on Towpath Road (near the double locks of the Erie Canal). Neighbors said that she built her hut facing the east where the sun rises. Dried corn hung from the ceiling, and outside, strips of meat hung on a line to dry in the sun.

An old ivy vine, gnarled and decayed at the roots, climbed half way up the stone chimney. Sometime back, the cold autumn frost had stricken the leaves from the vines until the skeleton branches clung bare to the crumbling stones. It's strange how everything looks different at night. Jenny's hut just seemed mysterious and intriguing in the daytime. At night it looked terrifying and dangerous.

Passers-by often complained that her window was so dank with mist that it was hard to see anything at all except the reflection of Jenny's own dark figure, hunched down under the dark green shade "spying" on them.

When the wind blew, every gust rattled the skull-medicine bundle hanging above her mossy green door.

She unrolled it periodically for ceremonial display. It was rumored she had in the bundle the head and shoulders of a hawk, a human skull, an eagle's claw and a deer's tail. All a symbol of bravery.

Jenny believed everything in the world about her was filled with spirits and powers that controlled her life, and she believed in performing a constant round of ceremonies to appease these spirits and solicit their aid.

Some of these rituals were wild and elaborate.

Her rituals and stories always provided entertainment and consolation to her neighbors. It helped the people around her to deal with their sorrows and their fears. Legends helped them explain and accept the calamities of life in a new land.

Jenny was also a storehouse of knowledge about a vast array of useful plants which could be used for medicine. Many settlers, like the Indians themselves, owed their lives to Jenny's medicine cure. Some plants she used for smoking, alone or mixed with tobacco, and most important for food.

The inside of her hut often filled with eye-stinging smoke. She smoked a pipe filled with tobacco she had grown in her back yard. When Jenny lit a mixture of tobacco and various aromatic herbs called "kinnikinnick" in the stone bowl of her pipe, her intent was deeply serious. She believed that the smoke that she exhaled was seen as a breath of prayer and the pipe itself was regarded as an intimate channel of communication to the spirit world. Although she grew most of her own tobacco, some of the tobacco smoked by the neighbors grew wild. Since raw tobacco tasted strong, she adulterated it with sumac leaves, bearberries and willow bark. My great-grandmother spoke of this to her children many times.

She smoked a pipe from time to time with Black Jenny, but didn't enjoy it, so she said. But at age 103, great-grandmother still would sneak a few puffs in the privacy of the outhouse.

Great-grandmother once asked Jenny where her husband was and she responded icily that she was married to a "warrior from the other world."

Being alone, Jenny had to find, grow and catch everything she ate. She became a great hunter and she used every part of the animal she caught. After she skinned an animal, she performed a simple religious ritual of respect —she would turn the head of the animal toward the east —the sacred direction where the life-giving sun arose and whence would come new life for the other game.

Immediately afterwards she started the tanning process. At first, this frightened the residents near her. She would stretch the fresh skin out on the ground, hairy side down, and peg it in place. Then working on the exposed side of the skin, she removed the meat and fat with a flesher, an adze-type blade lashed to an elk horn handle. Even her neighbors were a little shy towards her whenever she carried these tools about her waist. She finished with a stone scraper. As she worked she sang an eerie chant, like the sound of wind moaning through branches. No wonder children ran pell-mell past her hut. They were terrified of this strange old woman.

When Jenny made her own tanning fluid—basically, a concoction of the brains, liver and fat of the animal, the stench sent whitefolks turning away. Rather than pass it, they often fled from the place and took a detour home.

It was a long time before these early settlers understood Jenny's way of life.

Great-grandmother said that most women refused to

walk past Jenny's hut partly because she disliked children and partly because her Indian rituals often were misunderstood as witchcraft. She was thought to be able to exercise strong supernatural powers. Some say she used her power to foretell the future, find lost animals, bring good weather and even cast love spells.

Jenny explained her power came from a vision, a spirit in the form of a blackbird. It gave her power and told her how it was to be used.

Most of the whites feared her whenever she entered the spirited world, but often sought her help when in serious trouble. They wanted her services without having to be friends with her.

A strange tale told by many was that she had a doll made of animal skin and adorned with beads. One autumn evening, she used the sacred effigy to grant revenge. As darkness came on, Jenny threw new wood on the fire to make light for dancing. People, listening to her sounds carried on the night air, thought a giant carnival had come to town.

Gazing at the doll's face, she danced around the bonfire until she had a vision in which the doll told her, among other things, when and where she would die. The spell lasted for only one evening. The next morning, a boatman was found dead under the canal bridge and many believed it was the evil works of Jenny. Such an act seems out of character for Jenny, alive or dead.

When and where she died is a matter of debate. I cannot find any record of her even existing. I was tremendously excited to find somone other than my family who knew the story of Black Jenny. Marie, local historian, made me a map of the town that showed in detail where Black Jenny's hut stood. Surprisingly, I found that the

Devil's Hole—from the story of Great Uncle Frank—was near Jenny's land.

One rainy evening, Jenny failed to return home. That was in May; in November, a cold, unseen stranger, stalked about the canal roads, touching one here and there with icy fingers.

Shortly after her death, stories began to circulate in the surrounding countryside that her ghost had been seen outside her hut. Others declared that at sunrise they had seen her spectral figure in a canoe on the Owasco outlet.

An old canal resident told the story that, at about dusk one evening she was sitting in her rocking chair in front of the wood stove, waiting for her husband to come, when she heard Black Jenny's voice outside her door; and the awful baying of a ghostly hound. Shortly afterward, her husband arrived and, looking extremely pale, told her that he had seen Black Jenny near the livery stables.

Still on dark nights a mournful and dismal wailing noise is sometimes heard. Local people think it is the wail of Jenny's dog.

Many had the impression that something was walking immediately behind them as they passed her place.

For over a hundred years these stories were told.

In the late nineteenth century, a young wife of this area went to the canal bank to wash her clothes. As she worked, the woman glanced idly at the cool sparkling water and she stared . . . and stared. Floating on the surface, just off shore, was a deep and moving image of Black Jenny grinning, toothless, at her. Save for the tiny ripples of water that were left near the shore, it might have been a chimera of her idle brain. The frightened wife left screaming.

The apparition was seen, evening after evening, walking along the roads. It always approached from the east, lingered awhile in front of her hut and then glided away to the west, disappearing as it passed through the double locks.

One stolid and sensible villager was returning home by the old canal locks after midnight, having stopped at the Erie House for a few drinks. It was a calm and still night with heavy clouds obscuring the moon and he walked on in a happy mood when the quiet and peaceful night suddenly was shattered by the most discordant noises that he had ever heard. At first he supposed that a horse and buggy were near his side, but he only saw a black cloud. Through the drifting cloud, a ghostly old woman looked down on him and then moved across the road to vanish into the darkness of Jenny's hut.

The old hut stood empty, apart from its ghost, for many years. Some say she found it so comfortable she continued to haunt it nightly.

Local people were worried as to what would happen to Jenny's ghost when her hut was demolished. They need not have worried for the ghost was seen and heard long after all traces of the hut had disappeared.

Residents living nearby believed Jenny took revenge on her townspeople. Her ghost appeared and disappeared over the years to many as they traveled over the towpath road; but most believed she would never intentionally harm anyone.

Memories of her continued to stir fears in many families, but even the memories are now no more than scary tales.

Black Jenny had a great liking for one story and told it often, about a spirit that didn't scare her. . . . Perhaps, she has at last joined "her warrior of the other world."

2

Who Snuffed Out
the Candle?

It was 1890 when grandfather Samuel moved his family into the Mosher home on the west side of the village.

Their new home was very ordinary, a straight up and down sort of house, built on a hill overlooking the town. It was roomy and pleasant and there was a well-kept garden, with fruit trees, flowers and shrubs.

They were happy there until strange noises and happenings began occurring. As it was, grandfather continued outwardly to pay no heed, while seeking constantly to find some credible and rational explanation. To give way to fear would be to deny their faith in God.

The one thing that puzzled them principally was why did the children's room become the center of strange goings-on? Grandmother would put them to bed, cover them warmly with heavy comforters and, after kissing them goodnight, close the door behind her. Almost every morning she would be awakened by the cries of the children saying they were cold. Upon investigating, she would find the bed covers hanging out the windows.

At first she thought it was a child's prank, but they were too small to open a window, especially if it were locked. Being a devout Christian, she dismissed all supernatural thoughts from her mind.

This nightly disturbance continued throughout the winter and summer months. And things didn't get any better to say the least.

After the evening meal, it was the practice of the family to gather around the table while grandfather read the bible, but often the reading would be disturbed by crashings and stomping footsteps overhead. The more they ignored the noises, the more they increased. Then without any warning, the light from the kerosene lamp would be snuffed out.

On one horrific occasion when the light was snuffed and a spectral shadow could be seen moving slowly around the walls, grandfather, without a moment's hesitation, decided he must do something about this and right away. Everyone nodded nervously.

In his excitement his voice rose higher than he had intended as he explained his plan. He would sit up and watch closely to study this happening. Obviously somebody was playing tricks on his family, or else there was some architectural freak in the actual building, which caused nocturnal creakings or allowed the wind to create strange noises and blow out the lamplight when it blew in a certain direction. It could be some curious effect of light and shadow which doubtless could prove frightening to ignorant and credulous people, but not to a man like Samuel. He would solve this mystery and account for both the noises and apparitions in some perfectly rational way.

The night grandfather decided to solve this case, he wondered if anything untoward would occur. The disturbances peculiar to the house varied in frequency and intensity and it might well be that they would pass a perfectly peaceful night.

Grandfather knew he didn't have to worry about the children being frightened, because every evening he and the other adults told such amusing stories that they could hardly control their laughter. When the children went up to bed their minds were still full of jokes and pleasantries. They were so tired that they fell asleep almost as soon as their heads touched the pillows.

The house was still. The barnyard was still. Not a sound came from the street. Trizzy, the nursemaid, came into the room to tell grandfather that she would help him by sleeping in the children's room. He agreed that would be a double check and should be done. But he warned her to be careful and not let her imagination run away with her, as he suspected had often happened in the past.

Grandfather was studying the bible when suddenly something impelled him to raise his eyes from the page. The door of the stairway was opening very slowly. He sat motionless. He could feel the hair bristling on the back of his neck and a cold shiver ran down his spine. Slowly, slowly, the door opened and a gray shrouded figure emerged. Its hand extended, slowly, slowly, very slowly; noiselessly it advanced until it reached the kerosene lamp on the table. It paused and then snuffed out the light.

Grandfather gulped and shrank back. Suddenly he heard the pattering of bare feet on the floorboards overhead, yet there was no sign of the household awakening.

By now Trizzy had been awakened by a persistent knocking and then a hollow cough. The sound seemed to come from the closet. In spite of the warm summer night, she gave a slight shiver. After awhile she grew restless, stirred again slightly. Then she shrieked as she leaped under the covers. What she saw looked like a ghostly human shape with a snarled head and a long, skinny arm pointing out toward the lighted candle. Summoning all her courage, she peeped over the top of the sheet. Suddenly a violent gust of wind rushed through the room and in an instant the bed covers billowed out and then were swept right up to the top of the windowsill.

No sooner did the apparition disappear than Trizzy emerged from the huddled bed clothes, dressed herself quickly and ran from the room screaming! Still puffing she tried to describe the grotesque figure. She asked grandfather to rush at the menacing figure, but he couldn't see anything.

Trizzy experienced an eternity of agony almost too great for the human spirit to bear. It took many days before she recovered from her shock. She then begged Samuel, with a passionate earnestness, to never, never allow his young family to return to this haunted house. "Heaven preserve those little innocent children upstairs," she told him. "I'd have them far away from here if I had my way."

Members of the family on both sides were becoming increasingly critical. How could he subject his little ones to such ordeals? Trizzy now refused to sleep in the house, preferring to spend her nights undisturbed with the neighbors.

The heavy footsteps continued to noisily cross the

upper rooms and descend the staircase; doors opened and shut, mysterious knockings and movements were heard under the bed, and the well pump handle moved up and down without help, pouring water all over the yard.

For herself, Grandmother could accept this house and worse, but not for her children. Perhaps she was the only member of the family who knew for a certainty what "and worse" could involve. She alone had felt the touch of a spectral hand, ice-cold on her brow; first a sensation as of chilly breath, and then a steady pressure for what felt like an eternity, and then sudden release which left her sick and shaking. This was her great secret and telling the menfolks wouldn't change anything. They seldom made any comments except to condemn the ladies for being fanciful.

After this last ordeal, grandfather wrote down an account of these ghastly experiences and carefully preserved them in his bible, recording the curious happenings in this strange house.

He then took his family on a short vacation to visit his relatives in New York City.

They eventually returned to Port Byron, but grandfather had to move to another home for the sake of his children and also because of the notoriety which had destroyed the privacy of their home.

Some people came to the house out of curiosity, some seeking excitement, and some in a spirit of scientific investigation because they did not believe in ghosts.

One theory behind the strange occurrences was that a witch's cottage had once stood upon the site of this house and her malevolent spirit conjured up the evil doings of the past.

Others pointed out that those who refused to believe in the supernatural suffered most from the strange occurrences. The family of Samuel VanDitto, throughout their residence in the house, were subjected to peculiar horrors as if their resolute refusal to give way to evil atmosphere made them especially vulnerable.

Some Christians thought it was the ghost of a priest, who for some reason or another, had been unable to absolve the ghost of a terrible crime.

After grandfather's move, another family lived there but a short time, when the house caught fire. And this is another unbelievable story!

As the firemen climbed the roof of the burning house, they became suddenly pale. The flames around the chimney had taken the shape of a human figure. It rushed out and grabbed one of the fireman. His name was Rocky Russell, a distant relative of ours. He began screaming, "Help, help, something is pulling me down into the chimney." Only after a powerful struggle were the firemen able to free him.

The fire raged, but the haunted house would not burn to the ground. With great faith, grandfather suggested to the gathering of the townspeople that they pray for the soul of the ghost to find rest. At the end of the prayer, the flames died out and there remained only the crumbling walls of that ghostly house.

3

The Phantom in the Garret

One drearisome day in late October, Police Officer Tony received a call to investigate a landlady-tenant dispute. It took him several minutes to find the forlorn looking house because it was hidden behind a grove of pine trees at the end of a dirt road.

As he knocked on the old wooden door, which swayed precariously on a broken hinge, he thought this place has all the appearances of an Alfred Hitchcock thriller.

The door slowly opened and an elderly woman, in her late eighties, appeared. She seemed delighted to see him. He asked what the trouble was and she shouted, "HE is upstairs banging on the walls and disturbing me."

The officer asked, "You mean your tenant?"

"Yes, and that's not all. He never pays the rent, parties all the time and I think he's on dope!" she answered with indignation.

This last remark dictated an immediate change of strategy. Perhaps this was a more serious situation than a landlady's undesirable tenant. He feared things were about to start happening any minute. An old house in the middle of nowhere; an elderly landlady renting to a possible dope ring leader. Here would be a perfect hideout. This could be his chance to bust the flourishing narcotic business in his area.

He cautiously entered the room and asked, "Where is HE?" (She couldn't remember his name and referred to the tenant as 'HE'.)

Making muted unintelligent sounds, she hurriedly ushered him to the stairway.

The officer climbed a few steps and noticed undisturbed cobwebs floating above his head and dust covering the entire area. He turned to the old woman and inquired if she was sure someone was up there.

"Why of course! Can't you hear him banging on the walls?" she asked.

Listening and at the same time reviewing the stairway's untidiness, he calmly questioned her.

"When was the last time you saw him?"

She placed her hands on her head and sighed, "About three years ago."

Officer Tony realized he was getting involved in a strange case. He kept warning himself to keep an eye on this old lady. Is she acting irrationally or is there a corpse up there in the bedroom?

He started his climb and with every step had to wipe away cobwebs enmeshed with dead flies. Old stain-covered draperies hung crookedly from nails. This case was becoming more troublesome than he had anticipated. By now the questionable character behind him was following too closely with her heavy cane. Without thinking, he patted his holster.

Reaching the dark, timeworn room, he could see nothing distinctly. He turned to her and she was staring in the direction of an iron frame bed in the corner. Whole chunks of plaster covered a form underneath an old blanket. Tony now wondered if he had a homicide. There was no doubt in his mind that the corpse of the tenant lay there.

He unhooked his flashlight and made his way slowly to the suspicious looking body on the mattress. He poked his flashlight at the bigger pieces of plaster, causing clouds of dust to blind him temporarily. The old woman was hard to watch.

A thorough search revealed nothing but old pillows and blankets layered with mothballs. Tony sighed with relief.

"I don't think he is up here. Can't hear him. He's probably gone out to lunch," the young officer laughed, trying to reassure himself and wishing he had been investigating a barking dog complaint.

She stiffened her rounded shoulders and snapped, "Of course he is up here, you aren't looking in the right place. He is in there," jabbing her cane in the air towards the back wall.

Officer Tony decided to get downstairs fast and talk the situation over with her starting from the very beginning. He was almost as confused as he knew she was. In fact, he had to shake his head a few times to make sure he was awake and this was a true, live happening. And besides, he needed fresh air. It had turned into a very confusing afternoon.

Again he was convinced that one more discussion with

her would produce an intelligent solution to this bizarre case. He started the questioning and she immediately interrupted him with, "Would you like to meet my older sister?"

Of course, thought the officer, and waited for the invisible sister to appear, as he did for the upstairs tenant.

"Lenore, Lenore, come meet our nice visitor," she called out. To his astonishment, the dining room door handle began to turn. Then the shadow of a stooped-over woman appeared on the kitchen cabinets.

Lenore slowly approached the table and asked, "Would you have tea and cookies with us?"

TWO of them, he remarked to himself. He studied the sisters carefully. Never had he seen two more disarmingly, strange characters. He didn't have tea and cookies with them, but sat at the table hoping to wind up this call.

For the first time, Officer Tony noticed the table was set for three. Was there someone else in the family? No, the sisters informed him quite graciously; the setting was for the tenant if only he would come down from his room and behave.

Older sister, leaning right into Tony's face, asked, "Do you think we can rid ourselves of that pesky tenant? You know, officer, he is a Communist!"

Trying very hard to hide his broad grin, he asked, "Are you sure?"

"Oh, yes, and he carries a laser gun. We've seen it too. Every night he comes downstairs and zaps us with it," Lenore mumbled softly.

Younger sister complained, "My shoulder still hurts from last night's zap."

Officer Tony concluded he was getting nowhere with

these two ladies and should take his leave. Trying to do it politely, he made the mistake of asking the right time. Both of them pointed their canes toward a wall full of clocks, and shouted, "You tell us!"

He looked at the wall, then he shook his head in disbelief - every clock showed a different hour!

The old ladies gave a slight quiver as he stood up and started walking to the front door. One pulled at his arm and pleaded, "What about HIM?"

It was obvious now that he had to help them somehow before leaving, or face the possibility of returning again tomorrow.

"I'll straighten him out right now," he said. He put on his hat, swung his night stick and stomped up the dusty stairs.

"Look here, you," he hollered in his best command voice, "No more bothering these nice ladies and stop banging on the walls, or shooting your laser gun, or I'll be back for you. Understand?"

The two old ones were waiting for him at the bottom of the stairs.

"That's telling him sir," the sisters chorused, their heads bobbing like yo-yos on a short string.

When Officer Tony returned to his police car, he could see them standing in the dark shadows of the doorway, waving gaily to him.

What charming ladies, he thought, but they do have their peculiarities.

He heard a pounding noise as he went down the drive. Probably one of those loose shutters.

Or was it someone or something banging on the walls?

4

Francesco's Spirit

The scene admidst which Zuke told his story comes back very vividly to my mind. There he sat in his overstuffed easy chair by the spacious open fire, smoking one cigarette after another.

He always began an anecdote with a matter-of-fact air.

He puffed at his cigarette as though still hesitating about his confidence and said, "I saw a ghost once along the Towpath Road. It was around midnight when the R.S.& E. Trolley car dropped me off at Stop #73. Cousin Jim De Bottis and I had been to the Masonic Hall dance in town. Jim walked the short distance to his home. Luckily, I had carfare for my two mile ride because my head and feet were both giving me excruciating shocks of pain. Drinking too much hard cider behind the Carr building with the older boys and dancing all evening in new shoes almost did me in! I must say I was quite the dude in those days. I owned the only pair of black velvet pants in the county. Did I tell you my shoes were black patent leather, the high button style?"

He meditated more profoundly and continued:

"Well, as I started walking home from the high bridge across the Erie Canal, I saw a shadow of a man behind the telephone pole. At first I thought it was Francesco, and yelled out to him. He mysteriously disappeared. I stood rigid when he had left me, staring after, utterly mystified. Then there was a single piercing scream. For a split second I was frozen immobile. That was no ordinary ghost and something seemed to be telling me to get out of there quick. There was danger just being near this spirit, I feared.

"I forgot all about my hangover and tight shoes and mustered sufficient energy to race home. Finding the place in darkness, I shrank back against the front door in frenzied dismay. All this was very oppressive and after I stopped shaking, I lit a match and unlocked the door."

Zuke looked down at his cigarette and thought for a moment.

"That's all that happened for awhile," he said at last.

Zuke kept the secret to himself because he didn't want to upset the family with rumors of ghosts. Anyway, he never expected to see it again. He needed now to put the devilish experience behind him.

But, two weeks later, Cousin Jim had a similar encounter with the ghost. This time it was so viciously frightening that Jim refused to pass the canal bridge alone. To be sure, there were plenty of whispered rumors by now.

On two separate occasions, two months apart, witnesses reported hearing screams from the banks of the

Old Erie where earlier in the year, their friend Francesco had drowned. Most intriguing of all, was the fact that he had died a little before ten in the morning on the very spot cousin Jim had seen the image and just about the same time of day.

The ghost seen at the canal is typical of the ghosts of people who died in tragic circumstances. In some automatic way, they or some form of their memories seem to be attached to the scene of the tragedy.

Francesco's accidental death was the talk of the village for years. As the story is told, several young men were hanging around the canal bank planning a day of swimming. It was in the early spring and they all knew the water to be a little cold. They were still standing about trying to build up enough courage to make that first dive, when Father Cosgrove drove up in his buggy. It was said that he owned the fastest rig in town.

The young priest asked them to come to church, reminding all that it was the Lenten season and time for repenting. The boys listened patiently and then followed him to Sunday mass. All but Francesco, who laughed loudly, declaring to his friends that he was going to cool off in the canal. Francesco, alone now, dove into the canal water and was never seen again.

The Pratt brothers, with their rowboats and grappling hooks, searched for the body from High Bridge to the double locks. After the fourth day, the search was called off. Villagers believed the body was towed out of the area by one of the many boats passing through these waters.

Soon afterwards, ghost sightings and terrifying screams began occurring. Neighbors knew that this was indeed Francesco's spirit. A ghost in those days was defined as the spirit of a person no longer living. Soon fear took over the neighborhood.

Trizzy, the family nursemaid, had hung a "protection belt" of garlic around Zuke's neck and the smell of it seemed to fill the house and give the family members assurance. As you know, garlic is a wonderful protection against the more usual spirits or ghosts. Zuke hoped to be safe coming home from Saturday night's dance.

"We had a great orchestra playing that night. Dr. Stone's group from town. I should mention that Doc was a better dentist than a musician and I presume Alex, who played the flute, arranged all the music; he was that good. Would you believe the admission was twenty-five cents a head and well worth it. During intermission the ladies served coffee and sandwiches," he said with pride.

Before going to the dance, Zuke hid his garlic necklet underneath the trolley station and had plans to pick it up on his return trip home. He didn't want the garlic fumes to affect his social life.

It was in the very spot where Francesco had jumped into the canal, that Zuke came upon the ghost again.

Zuke said, in a tone of friendly superiority, "The ghost had his back toward me and I saw him first. He was very tall, had a meanish head with scrubby hair and rather large eyes; his ears were fanned out from his head like wings in flight. I wasn't a bit afraid, more surprised and interested, that is, until I discovered I had forgotten my garlic necklet under the trolley station.

"There we were, I and this thin, vague ghost, on that silent night, on that lonely road in the mucklands. Not a sound anywhere except my faint panting."

Zuke then stood up before the waning fire and smiled. He confessed at first he felt cold and nervous and had a prickling go up his spine and round his forehead from the back. But it didn't last long. He and Jim had been drinking again. This night it was homemade wine and he felt solid as rocks and no more afraid than if he had been assailed by their cat.

He reflected awhile, then continued.

"I say this in all kindness, but most haunting spirits are as stubborn as mules, to come back again and again."

"I knew him for a ghost, he was transparent and whitish, clean through his chest. I could see the glimmer on the window of Furry's house through his body."

Zuke's smile was frozen on his lips and he stood still. Then, he settled back into his chair and began again.

"That blessed ghost started talking to me!"

He looked apologetically at me, then, drew deeply on his cigarette and continued, "Mary Ann, I'm not joking."

He then emitted a thin jet of smoke rings which were more fascinating than his story.

From his account, it was a windy night with a full moon. A hound dog bayed somewhere near old Sam's house, making it hard to hear the ghost's words. Zuke took particular pains to saunter slowly and casually back to the telephone pole. He felt safer with something tangible between him and the ghost. In an instant the ghost was standing in front of him again, and no matter how he maneuvered, the haunt popped up. He could not get away, and what made it all the worse, was Francesco's spirit tried to start a conversation again. Then, for some mysterious reason, they seemed to be talking together as easily as if they had known one another all their lives. Zuke wondered if he shouldn't leave; he could think of better ways of spending his time than trying to make his life uncomfortable talking to a ghost he barely could see.

Little beads of moisture crept out all over Zuke's brow now. Oh, how he wished he had not forgotten the garlic! Oh, how he hoped there were still a few fumes wafting around him. Finally, he demanded in desperation, "What are you doing here? You weren't murdered here or something of that sort?"

The ghost, if possible, looked even more wretched. It moved closer; staring with those baleful eyes, it whispered in abysmal sorrow, "I drowned here."

To encourage the ghost, Zuke promised to bring the priest to this very spot the following Sunday after Mass.

Zuke hung me up again for a time while he sought matches in his pocket and lit another cigarette.

He drew on his cigarette and said, "You know, I never believed in ghosts or spirits before, ever, and then I meet one."

He regarded his cigarette ash thoughtfully for a moment. "That is all that happened," he said. "We parted and I kept my promise."

The legends have said of Father Cosgrove that he came to the canal bank mostly to console the grieving parents and relatives of Francesco. He carried a small gold cross and a bottle of holy water with him that day. He held the cross high, ceremoniously splashed the holy water on the surface of the canal and prayed: "Absolve O Lord, we beseech you, the soul of your servant Francesco from every bond of sin."

For a moment Zuke and I sat in silence. He welcomed the chance to think without interruption. Then he stood up and with trembling voice finally said, "Now listen quietly, I have something very strange to tell you. In the very moment of Father Cosgrove's concluding services, a strong breeze came up chilling everyone. The little group at the canal shivered. The ladies pulled their shawls closer around their shoulders. The men shuddered in their Sunday vests.

Then off in the distance, growing fainter and fainter, Francesco's scream was heard for the last time, and all present knew the spirit was gone forever."

Never again did the spirit appear to anyone. Francesco was absolved of all sin, it is believed, and now rests in his world of spirits. Or is this another of those inexplicable riddles that must remain unsolved until the end of time?

Tanner Dry Dock (boat repairs)

New Howard House

1916 - Pleasure boat made in Tanner's Dry Dock

.Kern's Lock Grocery Store (north side of double locks)

Port Byron Telephone Company Service truck

Saroney House on Erie

Conquest, New York

The Erie House
Peter VanDetto, Proprietor (white shirt) and his dog, Maude

45

5

Dr. Rabourn's Haunted Mansion

The year was 1939—just before World War II started. Everyone lived a fancy, fun-loving life. June, Casey, Billy, Agnes and I, just to name a few Port Byron people, still remember the good old days at Dr. Rabourn's home. A big, red brick, four-story, triple-stairwell mansion with many, many doors and windows.

Doc and his wife, Christie, had two darling daughters - Diane, the baby, age one, and Dolly, a beautiful child, age three.

Babysitting them was a happy time for anyone lucky enough to get the job and besides, the pay was excellent. That is until strange and mysterious happenings started frightening the occupants of this particular house.

The ghost in this mansion never rattled chains or flapped about wailing in misty sheets. All he did was come around sometimes when he happened to feel like it.

Reports seem to indicate that once he must have actually lived here.

It was strange that Doc never seemed upset by these doings and neither did his dog, a collie of gigantic size, named Beano. But the cat with the bulging eyeballs used to crawl away and hide, trembling with fear. Whenever wild rattlings were heard overhead, Doc would laugh and tease, "Just our friendly ghost."

After the bombing of Pearl Harbor, Doc left for the service. Christie and the children stayed alone in the house until pandemonium broke out almost every evening after she tucked the children into bed. Pictures fell off the walls, knockings were heard from the cellar to the attic, pans slipped off the gas stove and footsteps going up and down the backstairs shook the kitchen floor. Christie refused to spend another night alone and invited her sister, Marie, to keep her company. That worked quite well until one night when Marie was heading up the main stairs after a late date. A black derby hat sailed down past her head from the upstairs hallway. Marie cried out for help and her heart began to beat thunderously. She glanced frantically ahead and saw a spectral figure dressed in black coming down the winding stairway. The carpeted stairs could be seen through the figure. In an instant the ghost had melted into the darkness of the foyer. Marie slept with her sister that night and checked out the next morning.

My brother, Billy, was her replacement. He was going to high school at the time and agreed to spend evenings with the family.

There are occasions, particularly at night, when the air is alive with fantasy and even the most rational mind is tempted to admit the existence of the so-called supernatural. Billy tried not to be afraid . . . mainly because he was taking Doc's place as protector of his family. But after awhile he had to face up to the fact that something or someone was responsible for those strange happenings. He never bothered Christie with his fears and besides, she would only assure him that it was her father-in-law coming in the back stairs and going to his own room on the 3rd floor. Which reminds me of that special door near the back upstairs bedroom - always locked, and Doc warning all of us not to ever try to go in there. What was that all about?

Billy agreed that some of those noises might have come from the doctor's father - old Ossie, as we called him. He did visit the family at odd hours of the day and night and always seemed to be sneaking around the mansion. That might have dispelled some of the fears, but his stories about the live-in ghost and family curse from generations ago in Scotland only made the situation worse.

It was never worse for Billy than the night he heard the younger daughter, Diane, call from her bedroom for a glass of water. He was in the living room doing his homework at a huge Chippendale desk while Christie napped on a nearby couch.

Billy loved to run those glasses of water up to the children because he could slide down the banister when he came back downstairs. This time, however, as he headed up the steps, he heard the water faucet turn on in the upstairs bathroom, and a deep voice say, "I'll get you a drink of water." That puzzled him. No one was there but Christie and the children, and he soon dismissed it from his mind. Besides, no time now to scare himself, for baby needed a drink. Up the stairs he ran, taking two steps at a time. When he entered baby Diane's room, he really was shook-up, she was already drinking water.

He forgot the banister in his haste to return to Christie, who was still asleep on the couch.

He shook her to awaken her and the two of them began a systematic search of the house from roof to basement, where Doc had his office. They went all through the rooms to determine who could have brought water to the baby. They found no one, not even the baby's grandfather.

Things returned to normal, but Billy didn't sleep well from that night on. He soon decided to share that babysitting job with his closest friends. They all tried to ignore the noises and shadows in return for the good pay.

June, one of the last babysitters for the Rabourns, still remembers the scary times she had experienced there; especially the eerie feelings that would come over her whenever she entered those large drawing rooms. It was as if someone was staring at her and the chill of the air made her shiver. And this would be in the summertime with temperatures in the high 80's. I should mention here that it is a familiar phenomenon that haunted houses feel cold or chilly at times. No matter how high the temperature is in the rest of the house - even on a hot day - the cold spots stay cold.

The silver swords hanging proudly over the fireplace had a mysterious effect on June, as did the huge oil paintings of Mary Queen of Scots. We all were afraid to be in those rooms alone with the paintings. Mary Queen of Scots' large eyes seemed to follow the viewer from chair to chair or out of the room. Sometimes her facial expressions seemed to change and her eyes continued to look over our heads in a way as if they were smiling about some secret of their own. Doc's father explained that somewhere along the way, descendants of Mary Queen of Scots (which included the Rabourns) all were put under a mysterious family curse. He had the wildest stories concerning these descendants and their ghosts, but because of his peculiar personality, no one listened to him for very long and never believed his scary tales - that is until our lives seemed threatened by unknown and unexplained events occurring nightly.

Casey, another classmate who sat for the family along with Billy, had more spunk than most. Among the family heirlooms was a pair of sabres hanging ceremoniously on the wall. One night, finally sick and tired of all the rattling, rustling and wavering shadows, Casey pulled one of the sabres down from the wall and up the main stairs he charged to challenge the ruckus. Again, no one.

God-fearing Mary, the housekeeper, could easily sympathize with Billy - she had seen too much one night. She had read the older child, Dolly, asleep and was having trouble keeping her own eyes open. Suddenly, an old rocker in the room began swaying back and forth, back and forth. She could almost touch the heirloom rocker it was so close to her bed.

Shutters rattled outside the room. The darkness of the room was broken from time to time by pale shafts of moonlight as heavy clouds scudded across the sky. Shadows moved around for no real reason. And then, one of the shadows materialized, almost, into the figure of a wrinkled old man, rocking away in the chair. The voice of common sense kept making itself heard fretfully from time to time above the clatter of banging shutters. She put her head under her arm, hiding from the stooped-over old man's shadow near her bed. She tried to think of something pleasant, but the creaking noise of the rocker distracted her and she was forced to constantly check the rocker and shadow. When midnight struck on the grandfather's clock in the foyer, the shadow disappeared, and the rocking stopped, but the wind whistled through the shutters until early morning. Mary left the Rabourn household shortly afterwards; her encounter with a black shadow of a man in the upstairs hallway a few nights later prompted her into leaving without giving Christie any notice. She never came back - not even for a visit.

Things didn't get any better even after Beano joined in the game of trying to find the cause of these uncanny rappings echoing through the rooms.

It seemed impossible to escape from the old Rabourn mansion. In fact, it was impossible to so much as move from room to room without fatally attracting the attention of Doc's father or the ghost. They both had the eyes of a hawk and the ears of a lynx.

The times I remember most vividly are rainy days in that old mansion. When it rained and the wind blew, every gust made a noise like the rattling of skeleton bones and every step or bang echoed from floor to floor. Sleeping there was not easy. Nights would terrify even our friendly ghost, but when daylight arrived, that stately old home made us feel like royalty. Indeed, a beautiful ancestral place, but I must warn you, that of all the haunted houses in our area, this is probably one of the most ghostly.

After the Rabourns moved and the mansion was sold, I presume the ghost left too or is at peace with that old red brick structure on Main Street - or should I check with the present occupants?

Today, over forty years later, the ghost would seem to be still with us . . . especially now in October. He made his presence felt as recently as 1983, when the Crandalls owned the house.

Around one o'clock in the morning, he was heard playing the broken-down electric piano in the basement.

On another occasion, the oldest Crandall daughter and her girlfriend saw a figure, dressed in black, wearing a derby standing in front of the bedroom door. They screamed for help. Mr. Crandall searched through the halls with his loaded double-barrel shotgun in hand, while the other members of the family hid under cover. Not until daylight did peace reign in their household again.

Most intriguing of all, the image seen by the two girls resembles the one that Mary, the housekeeper, and Marie, Christie's sister, had seen many years ago in the same hallway.

Mr. Crandall, present owner of this stately mansion, threatened to put up a sign on the front lawn:

FOR SALE: Lovely brick home, complete with its own ghost, at no extra charge![1]

In October 1984, the Port Byron Elementary school children gathered at the old Rabourn Mansion. Mrs. Ann Kreiling, PROBE teacher for the school, Mrs. Kathleen Burke, audio-visual and video instructor, Mrs. Gene Crandall, present owners and I arrived to direct and film this ghost story.

We arrived around 9 o'clock in the morning. Mrs. Burke set up the camera and equipment in the large drawing room. From the very beginning she had mysterious problems.

The camera was battery-operated to make it easier for her to move from room to room and especially for the winding stairway scenes.

Mrs. Burke started filming the children and I outside on the front porch, followed us into the hallway foyer and into the drawing room. That is when strange things began happening to the camera.

THE CAMERA STOPPED WORKING . . . THE BATTERIES WERE DEAD!!!

"It can't be," she cried, "they are fully charged. I checked them at school several times."

Mrs. Kreiling and I looked at one another in disbelief. We couldn't possibly find another day suitable to all to make this movie. The children were disappointed too. They had been rehearsing their lines for weeks now and another delay would mean forgetting words, places, etc. Besides, the Rabourn house was vacant now and the spookiness of each room was more visible. Our last filming in 1983, had the Crandall furniture covering many of the hidden stairways and doors. This was perfect. Another problem - the house was sold and the new owners didn't know about their live-in ghost. Surely, we weren't about to tell them for fear the Crandall's might lose the sale.

Hesitantly, Mrs. Burke informed us it takes four hours or more to recharge the batteries. Then, she said our only solution was for her to go back to the school and get the electrical equipment and work the camera that way. It would hamper her filming in certain rooms, but she was sure she could get a long enough extension cord to reach most of the haunted places. We might have to cut out some of the scenes where no electrical outlets could be found.

While waiting for Mrs. Burke to return from the school with the electrical video equipment, Mrs. Crandall gave us a tour of the old mansion. She mentioned that she believed her daughters had played a trick on her recently. She had packed her pots and pans and had them stacked on the kitchen floor awaiting removal to their new home. The next morning she found all her pans back in the cupboards. She isn't sure, but when the daughters giggled, it may well be that they were the culprits. A last "house ghost" joke for Mom who had never seen nor heard it. She told us that she hated leaving this stately old house without at least seeing some signs of the ghost. The other family members had some terrifying experiences over the past sixteen years.

We all laughed and teased. Well, perhaps before the day is over, he will give a sign or even wave goodbye from the attic window, where the Rabourns believed he hid. The upstairs hallway is where most of the strange occurrences have been noticed. Most of us who knew of them would go out of our way to avoid walking through that section. Mrs. Burke set up her video equipment there!

Again, it would shut off inexplicably. Then, unusual accidents began to happen right before our eyes. . . . camera wouldn't work, cord kept falling off or out of the electrical socket, and enough of this scary business to make us peek around corners just in case he was toying with our patience.

Finally, the students, who were growing a little bored and perhaps tired of running up and down those many steps, tried a new approach—

Mrs. Kreiling and Mrs. Burke were kneeling beside the equipment on the upstairs hall floor trying to figure out the latest camera problem. I crouched down beside them and teased, "You don't suppose the ghost is doing this to us?"

They both laughed, but then looked up and I could see a "could it be so?" look on their faces. It was hard to believe that this equipment worked perfectly at school. Something or someone didn't want certain rooms filmed.

A new approach - even though the student felt strange about his actions, he walked to the attic door, opened it widely and yelled, "We know you are doing this. Please stop. We want to put this haunted house story on film TODAY."

After that, the camera started working again and we were able to finish the taping without any unusual difficulty.

We filmed the location where the ghost had been reported with some strange results.

When the tape was played back later, the voices were muffled and a great deal of noise had been picked up from somewhere. The children were quiet and the house was silent during the shooting. Was the noise coming from the ghost?

At the end of the filming, we gathered in the large living room where we had started. Mrs. Burke went over to the first camera with the dead batteries and was surprised to find the batteries working. They couldn't have recharged becasue it takes hours!

It gave us all the chilly-willys. Was the ghost still up to his old tricks? Did he grant Mrs. Crandall her wish after all?

---

[1] House sold October 1984; House returned to owner - Crandall;
For Sale sign up again October 1985; House sold 1986

6

The Devil Didn't Make Him Do It

I have heard many family stories and have enjoyed typing them up for future generations to read, but I must admit the strange happenings of Great Uncle Frank frightened me the most.

Great Uncle wasn't a bad guy, it was just that he kept bad company. That is what our relatives around this area were saying about a century ago.

And most unfortunately, some of that bad company included witches!

Even today our family doesn't care to talk too much about him, especially about the night he danced with the witches. They would rather point out some of his good traits.

Reading was one of those. In the early years of the Erie Canal, book peddlers from the big cities were always invading the small canal towns. Uncle was their best customer. He would drop everything on the farm whenever he bought a new book. Next to the black kitchen stove he would sit, to read it through to the final page. His books were demonstrably good and bad. Some say uncle would identify with the presumed hero of the book.

Great Uncle considered himself the local literary critic. After he read a book, he would either commend the literature to his many children or throw it in the stove. But not the Book of Commands given to him by a band of witches. He never spoke or paid any attention to his family while he was reading that Book. When he was done, it seemed evident that he had anticipated the devil. He could offer no explanation.

According to the story handed through our family, Great Uncle Frank was walking back to the farm one summer evening after attending a town meeting. It was hot and still. Heat lightning shimmered over the Seneca River. There was absolutely no breeze, however, and that is what made Great Uncle look twice when behind him a cloud of dust rolled up the parched road with a shadowy figure in the midst of it. It followed him to the forks in the road and disappeared before a blazing bonfire.

Through the drifting smoke several ghostly figures stared at him. It was August but he was shivering. All around the fire danced a band of witches. Uncle gulped and shrank back. Linking arms the witches did a grotesque dance of joy up and down the road, singing at the top of their voices. Uncle gazed at this strange scene with amused interest until they forced him to join them.

No one put wood on the bonfire, yet it never died down. He couldn't leave. Was he suddenly in danger? The darkness was highly sinister and even the moonlight seemed no friend. Several times he heard the neighing of horses. His eyes bulged out fearfully, searching for the sight of a democrat wagon.

At daybreak the witches stopped their wild laughter and crackling, turned and raced up the hill toward town. Great Uncle Frank stood there looking utterly beaten. He could see them huddled together as they passed the gray walls of the Erie Canal locks, and for a time was afraid they would return.

When he arrived home, his face was white and drawn. A bizarre night indeed, he thought. Even more so when he discovered the witches' Book of Commands, their own directory of spells, curses, and imprecations, in his coat pocket.

Night after night after that wild evening of dancing, he would sit in his favorite chair in the kitchen and study that Book of Commands. The family hated it. Reading from his Book of Commands brought cries of fear from them because of the many unusual happenings which often occurred.

After one of his readings, the children gasped in disbelief as the book leaped from the table. Great Uncle never had any problems turning the pages either—they would curl up under his fingers and turn themselves. Auntie had the most trouble with her husband and his Book and often left the room in tears. All the while he read, the lids on the old Andes woodstove shook and rattled up and down, sometimes spilling her cooking. Uncle chuckled at this. He knew then and there he could do anything he wanted as long as what he wanted was what the devil wanted too. The humor of the situation tickled the Italian in his soul.

It was a well known fact that Great Uncle had many problems with his sons. They sat in the shade of the barn most of the time. Work they seldom, if ever, touched. This will explain the next incredible chain of events, which to his family, was second in importance only to the Pledge of Allegiance.

Later that summer, Great Uncle stood in the middle of his fields looking in despair at all the work that had to be done before harvest. He had seven sons who were strong and healthy enough to tow a canal barge if need be, but they were lazy and shiftless, so grandmother told us. She would say in her sweet tone of voice, "Brother Frank's boys spend an awful lot of time doing nothing."

In desperation, he decided he could do nothing but command the devil for help. He remembered the special page in the witches' book. It guaranteed the assistance of the devil. Satan himself would come to his aid. All he had to do was ask.

Great Uncle Frank repeated the instructions. Nothing happened. Then he heard the unmistakable sounds of footsteps coming across his weed-covered ditches. He turned and there was a stranger, dressed "fit for the opera" but wearing a smile evil enough to scare fearless Great Uncle.

"Who are you?" asked Great Uncle as he looked him over out of the corners of his eyes.

"You called me, didn't you?" came the answer. "I am the Devil, at your service. What do you wish?" he asked in a tone of contempt and arrogance.

"I want all this farmwork finished, and now!" Great Uncle was gaining confidence.

"As good as done," smiled the "Ruler of Hell" through his grizzly black beard. "And all I want is one thing."

"What is that?" quavered Uncle.

"Only your Soul," returned Satan.

Uncle looked aghast. "My SOUL . . . NEVER."

The Devil's voice told him what sort of a satanic man he was meeting with. Great Uncle had to show him that he was still in control and could resist the temptation no matter how hard the work facing him.

"No," he cried. "Be gone."

He reached in his shirt, pulled on a golden chain and cross given him by his mother, Marguerite, and held it in the Devil's face.

The "Prince of All Evil" crashed to the ground and disappeared. He left behind only a widening hole in the ground. Steam and smoke poured out, then a stream of water filled the hole. And for year after year, that stream continued to flow. The hole grew wider and so deep that attempts to fill it with old railroad ties, boulders and tree stumps never succeeded. Some said that it once swallowed up a whole wagon with its team. Children were warned never to play near it.

The cavern was known by all as the Devil's Hole.

Finally, in the great flood of 1917, a torrential rain overflowed the Erie Canal and when the water went down, the Devil's Hole was gone.

And the family, who had whispered for generations about Great Uncle Frank and his dance with the witches, smiled knowingly and said, "Yes, he was known to skip the truth for a brief lie; but no one doubted his story of his encounter with the Devil!"

7

Spook Woods

On a chilly autumn evening, many years past, a curious little drama unfolded against the placid setting of the hamlet of Pepper Mill. This town was an outskirt not only of Port Byron, but of civilization!

It happened so long ago that most people have forgotten it. The name seems exact, though, but no doubt the details have changed with the disappearance of the town. They all tell the same tale of the forest-dwelling witch of Spook Woods.

Almost every full moon night, the villagers could hear what sounded like hoofbeats in the cemetery. So real did they seem that some of them went up to the cemetery the next morning, after such a bizarre evening, to look for the hoof marks of the horses and it was shocking to them to find not one foot-print on the grass or dirt road.

Shortly after these occurrences began, an old witch-like woman dressed in ash colored clothes and wearing a ragged burlap shawl thrown over her head and wound once around her neck, started shopping at the local grocery store. It was the only store in town. Theo, a devout churchman and one of the founders of the town, owned and operated the small business. Soft-coal and tobacco smoke filled the building. Villagers used the place for meetings and to swap bits of news.

Theo was the only one who would talk freely about the old woman. He told his grandchildren that the old witch rode in a wagon drawn by a black horse whose mane and tail were white. She never spoke to anyone and no one spoke to her. She would buy her supplies, pack them into her shabby, capacious leather sack and leave for her home deep in the woods.

She lived a solitary life, as might be expected, for few cared to risk being friends with her. A sooty-feathered crow, who talked from dawn to dusk, was her only companion. Most villagers feared this harsh-of-voice bird, for it was believed to be a messenger of death. If it flew around the window, croaking, it meant death to a family member inside the home.

This region produced a race of men and women who were very strong and fearless, but on the night of the full moon, they huddled safely in their homes. Besides, no one could tell when disaster might strike. Most of them believed that hidden among themselves were black witches, who could command destructive winds and rains, destroy crops in the fields and cause harm or death by the power of a glance alone - the EVIL EYE!

It's no wonder when unexplicable accidents occurred, the people of Pepper Mill looked for malice nearby in Spook Woods. By one means or another they traced the evil works to the black witch of the woods.

On the witch's first visit to the store, she pulled out her money to pay for her groceries and a small bundle fell out, dropping bones and potent herbs to the planked floor. A few dirty hemlock twigs drifted onto the counter top and around the customers standing nearby. The hideous old hag leaned toward them and gave all a grin full of evil. No one moved or said a word until she left with her bag of things and her wicked grin.

Theo said that last time the old woman was seen leaving town, she turned and looked at them with an expression of great sadness and then quickly disappeared into the darkness.

There were many such incidents.

One man told the incredible tale of riding with the old witch one stormy night. Up the road came the sound of creaking axles. He stopped and turned to look and, although it was growing dark, he could make out the vague shape of a horse and wagon coming toward him. He waved his arms and shouted. The driver did not answer, but the wagon came on swiftly, bumping along over the ruts in a careless way. Then suddenly the old witch, revealing ferocious teeth, yelled "Whoa, you black beast," and stopped at the cross-roads and offered him a ride. I should mention here that most hauntings occur at cross-roads because witches are supposed to have used them for such purposes.

He turned to look at the ghoulishly wrinkled old witch who was humpbacked, thick featured and smelling of the forest, and what he saw took the words out of his mouth. He was about to ask her to slow down. It wasn't so much the sight of her, although that was bad enough, but she was the hairiest creature he had seen in his life. A thatch of wolf-black hair grew over her head, down her short, fat neck and almost covered her face and hands. It blew wildly in the wind. She looked like a frightened beast dressed in shabby clothes.

It was whispered that this witch had a magic bridle. It was made from old bones and flayed skin of corpses— whose, no one will ever know. It was the bridle of a super- natural being. When flung over the head of a horse, the bridle made that beast fly as long and as far as the witch commanded. He was sure this was true because he had felt the wagon wheels leave the ground several times already. Besides, her horse, unaccountably heedless of the rein, had taken them on a demented gallop through every ditch and stream along Spook Hill Road. He was terrified and eager to escape from her as soon as possi- ble.

As they winged homeward, he plucked up his courage and jumped off the speeding wagon to freedom. He landed on his hands and knees. By the time he pulled himself together and stumbled to his feet, the old witch was out of sight. He could hear the horse's hooves pounding down the other side of Spook Hill Road. Still he couldn't move, couldn't force his mind to accept what the eyes saw. When he realized how bizarre these hap- penings were, he shrank back in wretched terror.

Even by day Spook Hill Road, which wanders away up towards Spook Woods at the north side of the village, was seldom used; and then only by strangers who had never heard of the witch.

Of course, if a stranger had been foolhardy enough to want to go over Spook Hill Road on a full moon night, the villagers would have done their best to hold him back. But by good fortune, strangers were few, and villagers seemed contented to travel by day.

It stunned the townspeople when they heard that the old witch caused two men, who apparently tried to follow her home, to be spirited into a ditch along side of Spook Woods. They were found the next morning, bound together but unharmed.

After that last incident, matters escalated until the neighbors together tried to follow her home.

It was a wild night. An owl's screech echoed through the pines and a few black clouds covered the full moon from time to time. The leaders of the town went around the village calling all the men out of their homes to come with them to hunt the old witch. It helped a bit that the doctor led the way with his horse and buggy. He thought someone may get hurt which was why he went along. The doctor put no stock in ghosts and witches and said so bluntly.

They found the path into Spook Woods easily enough, and how could they miss, with every man carrying a lantern and with the full moon riding the sky and flooding the road with light.

Some of the women pleaded with them to turn back. The ordinary rigors of travel were daunting in those days. A journey to another town could take many hours or several days over rough roads under the best conditions. But most often they encountered muddy roads and swollen streams and misfortune could strike at anytime. Spirits and witches could bring about all these things and more. Their favorite way to display power to travelers was to mislead them. Some used mimicry to confuse the villagers, others appeared as old women and they all disliked mortals.

There are conflicting tales about that witch hunt into

the woods.

One of the villagers called to her, "Come out." Then, made reckless by curiosity, he strode to the first pine tree.

"Come out," he said again. A burst of evil sounding laughter was the only reply. Suddenly, the one-eyed witch stepped lightly into the road and stood before them. It was said that one of her eyes closed and withdrew until it was almost invisible, while the other opened until she was one-eyed. The silent crowd saw her pet crow pause by her side; then a mist arose around her as she walked into the woods. No one ventured to follow her at that moment.

The tall trees of Spook Woods grew in multitudes so dense that in Pepper Mill, it was said, a squirrel could hop from one end to the other without touching the ground.

When the townspeople entered the woods, they knew at once that this was no ordinary place. The trees were thick with leaves and their branches swayed gently, although no wind stirred. After the men had walked some little distance, the woods thinned and the fog became dense. There was a hooting, inhuman whistle coming from far away through the woods. One of the men could see the old witch trudging slowly along the path, waving her bony fingers summoning them. But though they quickened their steps, they drew no closer. They sped on, too terrified to tire or to even look back.

How far they had traveled in this miserable woods no one could tell. The ground passing beneath their eyes changed from leaf-littered forest to boggy marsh and the air grew steadily colder. Almost at once they halted. They were lost! The forest was almost gone and in its stead was the swamp. Only when the ground beneath their feet grew soggy, did they realize that in their single-minded pursuit they had strayed far from the main road and blundered into quicksand territory.

Swiftly and methodically the witch moved among the fir trees and brush. Suddenly, chilling screams of laughter rang out. The hideous sound filled the woods and they knew now that the witch had tricked them.

Remembering the witch's destructive powers, they needed protection at once. One man knew the ancient phallic gesture and quickly outstretched his arm, then the hand with its inner fingers curled and its two outer ones stiffly extended. Another drew out his hunting knife knowing witches often feared iron. The laughter stopped.

It is no wonder that strange tales about unseen powers were at play in those days.

The men now were hopelessly lost in the dark and there was nothing to do but wait out the night in that forsaken swamp and woods. Fortunately, their adventure had a happy ending: they all returned home safely.

A few old timers with a taste for enchantment, who remembered the witch's trips into the town, refused to discuss or even admit that she existed, but do eagerly tell of the problems they had keeping a clergyman.

Some of the clergymen who lived here reported strange happenings around the church grounds, adjoining the cemetery. Most of them and their families, who might have remained longer, left after only a brief stay, unable to cope with the place.

Many of the incidents at the cemetery seemed to involve the mysterious old witch. According to the story that is told, and no tale could be more unlikely, I must admit, on the day the old witch disappeared into Spook Woods and never returned, her spirit sallied into the cemetery, down the graveled path to the iron gate where she and her horse and wagon swept on through all the headstones. It was quite noiseless.

Her appearance was said to have been witnessed by several mourners standing by a grave.

Hunters today are often startled to hear phantom screams breaking through the forest stillness.

If the reports of recent visitors to Spook Woods are to be trusted, she may still dwell there!

8

Lobo

The villagers said that most of the stories of werewolves and ghosts were told by people who were poor and uneducated. They had many other superstitions as well.

But in the small settlement west of town, the frightened residents knew better. Something inhuman had come to their area. They were not uneducated people; a doctor, two teachers, lawyers and farmers were all neighbors. And they were not being fanciful.

They lived in a relatively peaceful age. It was the autumn of 1915. Nobody knew how soon the war would come and they did not worry about it. They were peaceful times now. Strange that such horror could be born out of such peace.

This episode began late one evening when the full moon painted the darkened houses of this sleepy canal town. Something strange started to howl. From their porches, neighbors could hear the animal-like cries. At first they didn't know where the sound came from, it was everywhere! Terror-stricken, they clutched one another for protection as the howls became louder and more terrifying. Children already in their beds screamed and pulled the covers over their heads. The noise was very distressing. A second night passed in the same way as the first, and a third.

It was a scene repeated many more times. Thus began the years of the howling wolf-man of Port Byron.

Lobo was a wolf-man or werewolf, call it whatever you like. He had known it for a long time and so had his family. NOW his new neighbors knew it.

They were a strong and close-knit people and they gathered around their friends in times of need. People's lives revolved around those of their near neighbors. However, in this case, when they heard Lobo's terrible wolf-cries swirling around on nights of the full moon, they dispersed to their own homes. The children were sent to bed. Their doors were locked and everyone prayed for the wolf-man's soul.

Accounts of Lobo are sketchy and contradictory having come down from local story tellers.

It was whispered that he was of fairy lineage. That story began in Europe. Some letters said that because of the timing of his birth, he was destined to be a werewolf and all the villagers knew it.

Lobo said, "This was nothing I asked for. I wasn't bitten by a wolf or cursed by a witch. I was born in the high mountains of Italy where wolves ran freely, where wolves howled at the moon every night. Perhaps that was when it started to happen. I was always mimicking the wolf cries and I soon became a fanatic."

But relatives said that when a baby, his parents rubbed him down with wolf fat to keep his skin soft and then he became a werewolf.

Whatever the cause, he was nicknamed "Lobo" by his people. (Lobo means "wolf or timberwolf"). This name came to him as a child and followed him to America. He claimed he was baptized "John" but there is some question about this - was he baptized?

As a child he was a sensitive, imaginative little boy, always surrounded by influences which turned his imagination into the paths of the most unwholesome superstitions. But beyond the beliefs of most of his relatives, in his own nature he was keenly appreciative of the wolf. For Lobo there was a wolf cry in every wind rustling the tops of the trees.

Lobo's village was beyond the main mountain range of the Alps. The journey there entailed many hours of steep climbs and almost vertical descents over a series of razorbacked ridges, plunging ravines; the whole way through dense forest. Lobo loved his wilderness home and his friends, the wolves.

Years ago countryfolks who believed in werewolves thought that they looked like real wolves; but the people around here, thought of something else when they heard their werewolf; they thought of their friend and neighbor Lobo. They said he was a hairy creature that walked on two legs like a man and made wolf sounds only when the moon was full. To some it seemed natural when he changed from man to howling wolf at full moon. Wolves were supposed to howl at the moon. But most of them were filled with fear.

Because Lobo's eyebrows grew together, many suspected him of being a werewolf long before the first dreadful howls arose from his porch. They said Lobo was a werewolf who wore his wolfskin on the inside of his body. When normal, he was a good man, and they tried very hard not to forget it.

According to a few inhabitants of that time in history, Lobo was a giant of a man. He stood six and one-half feet tall with a thick tuft of black hair on his head; his great arms swung at his side as he walked and his large hands almost touched the ground. He weighed two hundred-fifty pounds and wore a size thirteen shoe.

He was in his middle years when he moved his family to the Houghtaling Farm. He rented the tenant house located on the south side of the Erie Canal. Their home was sparsely furnished but spotlessly clean. He was poor but proud.

He worked on the mucklands for VanAcora. He had a good work record, many friends and it was said that the pace of his work was superhuman. He could cultivate an acre of celery in half a day. VanAcora was lucky if his other workers could do it in two days.

On some days, usually when the moon was full, Lobo knew that he felt good and exceedingly strong. This feeling, however, ebbed with the moon, and then grew again with the next moon. He learned to detect the signs that foreshadowed transformation, as slight as his was, and so did his family.

Usually victims of this curse prepared secret rooms in their homes and locked themselves in when the time approached. Lobo didn't need this treatment, not yet anyways.

As the story is told, it started three days before the full moon. He felt familiar sensations. A great restlessness. He was afraid of his world and what he might do. This year was not like the others; strange shadows in the moon frightened him.

A terrible compulsion drove him out of bed. His wife regarded him for a moment with narrow suspicion before going back to sleep. He felt the coldness of fear probing just below his heart. With a tremendous effort of willpower, he tried to walk back towards the bed but some cataleptic spell made him helpless. He could not stir, he could not even speak.

As the full moon came out from behind the smoky-gray clouds, it added a sort of terror to the countryside. Moonlight can be eerie. It is unnatural somehow, and some believe there's a lot in what they say about there being evil in the moon. There is an old superstition that some people went crazy when the moon was full.

As Lobo's eyes roamed around the ill-lit room, he discovered that the moonbeams were entering the bedroom window. He sensed their power. He did not want to change into a howling wolf, but there was nothing he could do about it. He believed he couldn't even kill himself; werewolves are immortal.

He sensed the moon somewhere over his rooftop. With one convulsive movement he thrust at the latch of the door. His growls swelled and slowly grew louder and louder. He gazed out into the darkness beyond the porch for a moment and seemed to scent the air. He groped at the porch railing, bellowing wolf-cries of rage. He was hunched over but he was clearly not a werewolf.

Family members could hear his phantom cries rising, it seemed, from the walls. Others heard as well. His closest neighbor, Cabby Young, heard him screaming and when he looked out of his window, could see Lobo standing in his longjohns - alone in his wolf world.

No one dared to venture out into the night. His shrieks battered the windowpanes; they went crazily on and on, punctuated by gasping breaths. Every man and woman in this canal town that night knew that wolfman would terrorize them with his howls until daylight.

The wind blew steadily, beating branches against the house, rattling doors on their hinges. Over all this and over Lobo's mad howling his wife heard him calling for help. Reacting quickly, she rushed outside and found him shivering in the cold, his bare feet buried in the snow. His pleasant, remarkable face was somehow shifting, stretching and there was a vital similarity to the snarling face of a wolf.

Suddenly, Lobo felt like a wild animal. Surveying his wife with dull empty eyes, he swung around and struck blindly at her. He missed. After that he stood quite rigid. His flannel shirt was stretching, stretching and the shirt's seams began to pull apart. With a guttural cry, he lunged in every direction, swinging his arms ferociously; then he began to shake visibly. His breath came and went in spastic seizures. At last dropping to his knees he crawled further out into the snow. There was another terrifying wolf-cry. The moon was the last thing he recognized.

The air grew steadily colder and the snow fell, first in large flakes, then in a shifting veil of white powder. Lobo's wife forced herself to be calm. Looking up into the heavens she did not feel the least bit afraid. She saw only the beast that lurked within him. In truth, she felt exasperated about what was happening with her husband and to her family. He had embarrassed them so many times until they could not stay in one place for very long. But most of all he kept them in a bondage of terror for years on a full moon night.

Her tears, mingled with snow, streamed down her cheeks. She tried to restrain him but he pushed her away. In spite of all this roughness, she never gave up but continued to display her customary gentleness to him. She wanted to cover him with a blanket and lead him back indoors, and again he shook her off howling with fury.

She was a practical woman and she felt no anxiety about spending the night in the open with him. She wrapped herself in the blanket and settled nearby, praying this nightmare would end soon. He continued until morning, his screaming wolf-cries quivering in the cold night air.

When dawn appeared, Lobo's wife seized him, led him inside and he fell limp into the bed. He gave a wailing sigh before falling instantly asleep.

It was quite bewildering. He always remembered falling asleep in his bed, but had no memory of waking and walking out the door into the night.

Lobo's knowledge of what he was began to make him realize that something must be done about his condition. He was a victim of an evil his family and friends could not understand. For the first time he seemed to be looking realistically at his doubtful future. New lines of worry deepened around his eyes. One day he told his story to a wise old fortune-teller of the village and that night acted on her advice.

She believed the curse could be broken by measures that required steadfast courage on the part of his family, who had to look directly at his eyes when he began his wolf-cries and call him a WEREWOLF! Risking bodily injury from his wild actions, they called him a werewolf over and over again. It didn't "take"; then they sprinkled him with holywater. Nothing happened.

Soon afterwards a witch doctor came to visit him with her bottles of noxious medicines; possibly his neighbors had sent her. Lobo sent her away with an outburst of howling cries that only a wolf could appreciate. She made the big mistake of making a house call on a full moon night.

He was never freed from his animal cries and the curse that circumscribed his life.

Tales of Lobo were told in homes, saloons and almost everywhere throughout this region long after he and his family disappeared the night of a warm-weather moon (bloated and orange-colored instead of cold white).

Just as people said, Lobo yelled out across the mucklands many years after his reported death. As recently as the forties. Billy and Barb, my brother and his wife, heard wolf-cries on the nights of the full moon during their brief stay on the Houghtaling farm's big house.

No one would live in the tenant house after Lobo. It was too dark and cold and still. Those who passed by at night said that they had seen a pale werewolf on the porch staring at them.

This story ends with the rumor that after Lobo's death, his wife had him cremated.

She feared he would become a vampire after his death. It was "common belief" in those days.

Pine Hill Skull and Glob

It is believed that the older the story the more ghostly it will be, but that is not the case. The more modern, the more ghostly it is; the nearer it comes to the reader, the more it strikes him.

This is a haunting I have looked into myself and gathered all the facts here noted. I have eliminated place names and family names in order to spare the present occupants of this haunted house from sightseers. The alterations are slight.

It was the folks who live in this house who started all the talk about an unidentified glob and a "moving" skull.

As Iggy tells it, he was alone. The house was so quiet, so utterly hushed.

When the door began to creak, he called out to his wife, "Marie, is that you?"

No answer. He began reading his paper again. Suddenly, the living room door creaked but this time it opened wide enough for him to look out into the next room. He gave another call to Marie, even though he knew she was still out shopping. Perhaps, he thought, she had returned earlier than usual and he hadn't heard her. He checked the adjoining rooms and behind the door. He could see no one, yet he felt the presence of someone in the room. A cold and eerie feeling came over him. When it happened again, the door creaking and closing behind him, he started a thorough investigation. This was making him extremely nervous.

He ran to the front of the house and looked out. His look lasted no more than a moment because, out of the corner of his eye, he saw a strange thing begin to happen to the wall clock. The hands turned round and round. Now this whole thing had an air of unreality.

Something inside was telling him that, if he didn't panic, this problem would be solved. But soon he thought he heard rappings, scrabbling and, worst of all, the click of teeth near the entrance to the room. When he glanced in that direction, he saw only an empty archway.

He could see the curtains between the rooms moving as if someone or something had just passed through.

He quickly returned to his chair and began to fiddle with his eyeglasses.

Through the slit between the door and the jamb a shadow appeared, no thicker than a sheet of paper. It moved to the center of the room. The outlines were blurry. Iggy rubbed his eyes and looked away. He wasn't going to think of it anymore. Probably a temporary delusion.

Before settling back down to his reading, he gave a

quick look over his shoulder and that ugly sight has remained in his mind to this day.

Appearing on the living room rug was a huge, colorless glob. What was happening here . . . what a mess . . . and what was it? It must have worked its way up from beneath the floor, he thought.

He didn't believe in spooks and specters, in devils and moaning or creeping things, but this was enough to get the better of anyone.

There was a horrible fascination about the ghostly glob quivering on the rug. It had no definite shape or color and he couldn't describe it as anything he had seen before anywhere—not even in the movies.

He passed a shaking hand over his eyes. He held perfectly still, every sense straining, alert. Then he walked a slow circle around it; shuffled unwittingly down to it; dropped to his knees and grovelled apprehensively on the soft carpet. He cursed it. How could he explain this mess to his wife. She would never believe it anyway.

Frantically, his fingers slid over it in a hectic effort at appraisal. Was that glob evidence of extraterrestrial visits to earth? Or was it this old house? It was full of queer noises because of the foundation settling. Several times they had heard disturbances coming from the dining room like the sounds of chairs being pushed back from the table but every time they checked, the chairs were in place.

Iggy now had control over his emotions and grinned. "Hell, the answer is simple - broken pipe in the cellar. I'll check it out."

Returning, his expression blank, he looked over at the frightening glob, then quickly put his arm around the empty chair near him to steady his now shaky legs. He sipped on his cold coffee and sat there in semi-darkness and silence for a long while. Was he losing control of his senses? Did he experience all this or was it a bad dream?

That last hour was the longest in his life - alone with a ghastly looking glob.

From a distant room came the sound of the door closing. Marie had come home at last. He called to her in a hoarse, cracked voice. "Come in here quickly, you can't imagine what has happened to our rug!"

His throat was so dry he could barely swallow. He squinted through sweat moistened eyes at her.

"You can't imagine what it's been like, I've had it all," he told her.

Marie's eyes uneasily searched the dimly lit room for an answer. She sank into a chair as though the strength had gone from her body. But being blessed with a good brain, an abundance of common sense and a liberal dash of pluck, agreed to assist him in solving this mystery. She warned him that they might see something that they both would wish they hadn't seen. Marie always broke the mood with her laughter and Iggy began to relax again.

Iggy gave me the briefest mechanical smile, then continued his story.

"The glob did vanish," Iggy explained. "It shrank and shrank, then melted into the darkness of the room, leaving no trace or evidence that it had ever slithered around on the rug."

He wasn't afraid of this old house, the Dr. Gilbert home, but more strange happenings were occurring regularly. It wasn't the sort of home you'd think would attract a ghost. It was far too neat and pretty for ghosts to care much about. But, nevertheless, strange events in this household began in the 1980's and maybe still are taking place. Iggy isn't saying one way or another at this particular time.

Dr. Gilbert was the old time practitioner - seen everywhere at all hours of the day and night going to and from households. Some dared to say, distributing mostly his sugar tablets. But others claimed he was a super doctor and could cure almost anyone for the small fee of $1 per housecall. He rented a horse and buggy from Newkirk's Livery Stable located on Utica Street for $1 a day. Doc was the town's homeboy - who graduated from Port Byron Academy - even pitched ball for the home team.

He kept very busy caring for the townspeople and many times went to bed with his trousers and his hat on. There was general belief that his mare slept between the shafts of the gig with the bridle shoved up on her forehead.

Dr. Gilbert's study of brain anatomy may have been the reason the skull in the attic was never taken out of his home after his death. A reminder of his great contribution to medicine.

It was rumored that he had a collection of bottles high on a shelf in his office that were the grizzly contents of the human brain. Whose? These were acquired, post mortem, with the consent of those to whom the parts once belonged, I am sure. Little harm had been done and perhaps, in the long run, some significant human good. Doc lived with his collection. It didn't bother him or his patients. Why should we now be squeamish today? There is a lurking fear that some things are not "meant" to be known; some inquiries are too dangerous for human beings to make.

It took Iggy time to stammer out the words, "My attic is haunted, I'm sorry to say."

I smiled inside, but didn't change expression, just shrugged.

"Mary Ann, I have told this story so many times that now I am afraid people will start saying I am getting senile and I am only in my early sixties, remember?"

Naturally, he did not expect to be believed, and he did not mind whether he was or not. He did not believe in ghosts but the thing happened and he proposed to tell it as simply as possible.

Soon after the doctor's death, Iggy and family moved into the doctor's home. All the doctor's possessions were given away or sold - all but the skull from the office. It was taken to the attic and placed as a ghoulish center-piece on the shelf. It remained there, quiet, night after night, for many years until several months ago.

Iggy walked toward me and in a tranquil tone said, "Recently, that skull has started moving to the end of the shelf - sometimes falling to the floor."

His wife leaned forward eagerly and tried to shush him.

He shuddered and fidgeted with his feet. "I don't like that skull at all," he confessed. "What big eyes he must have had. No one is able to offer final proof, but the skull may well be that of a patient," he teased.

At first Marie laughed when he told her that he had imagined the skull moving whenever he entered the attic. But one day, she heard it hit the floor and now refrains from any comment.

I asked if I could see the skull: This was unbelievable and I needed to prove to myself that ghostly incidents can happen in my time.

It was difficult, after viewing it, not to wonder whether in some sense the patient was still in there. It was enough to give one the creeps even in the daytime. I found the attic eerie and uncomfortable. How could Iggy spend the night in there? He did, as the story goes.

Iggy felt that everywhere he walked in that attic the skull's eyes followed him. I decided to leave immediately and hear the rest of his experiences with the skull - but in the living room! It was good to be out again into the sunlight. I gave the rug a quick yet thorough once over. I didn't expect to find anything and I wasn't disappointed.

Iggy thinks he may have caused the episode. He decided to rid the attic of some junk including the skull so he moved it to another place. It stayed hidden back in a dark corner of the room only a short time.

One evening shrieks were heard coming from the cemetery in back of their home. But worse awaited them, for one morning their garden was ruined - all the plants destroyed. Some of his closest friends were half convinced already that they knew the truth; that something not quite human, indestructible and totally evil was walking the cemetery at night. But Iggy knew better. He immediately dug the skull out of the dark corner, cleared the cobwebs and dust from its eye sockets and returned it to its rightful place. Peace returned but its movements along the shelf continued. Once again the skull had bent mortals to its implacable will.

Iggy wondered if he should risk an attempt to stay a night in the attic. Marie thought it was a crazy thing to do and warned, "You'll have more than one optical illusion before this night's out, I expect." But he was getting stumped and ready to try anything.

"To tell the truth, I felt a little scared," he said, but there was nothing to be afraid of, he told himself. It was just an old attic. The wallpaper had some crazy cracks running every which way through it; other than that it was just another room used mainly for storage.

It was his objective to find out for sure, if that skull really moved.

He went up in the darkness and felt his way to the attic and then to the small window inside. His brow, cold with sweat, he felt his way round the room and groped along the wall until he found himself with the skull in his hand.

He sat near it until he was chilled with the cold, glancing occasionally at it. He needed a cup of hot coffee.

It suddenly struck him that, in the time he had left the attic and returned, there had been a subtle change in the skull's position. It seemed to have turned at least one degree to the left. He had neither seen nor heard a movement but it was as if some sixth sense had made him aware of one.

Iggy now knew that once he took his eyes off the skull it took advantage of it to shift its position.

He swung himself around so as to bring himself face to face with that dreadful skull. "YOU MOVED, blast you, you did, I SAW YOU!" he cried out.

Then he stood still, staring straight ahead like a frozen man. Alone in the dark, he knew he was going to have a few bad moments.

Maybe at night, the dark aura of the room was playing tricks on his mind. He was going to have to sit tight. He was terribly afraid but he would not admit it to his wife.

He thought there was no guarantee he would be able to do a damn thing if the skull moved.

A stray beam of moonlight slashed through the clouds and glinted off the window sill. Shadows forming on the walls added a certain ghastliness to a scene that needed no additional touch of horror.

The door banged, he thought. At first that was what it had seemed, but the sound came from the shelf. He turned sharply and started running over the dark, cluttered attic, which he knew like the back of his hand. That skull had fallen off the shelf again!

Iggy had tasted danger during the war years and found it not to his liking, so out the door he ran. He went as rapidly as he could, deliberately trying to leave that noise and the skull behind.

He stopped abruptly at the bedroom door and asked, "Hear that?" Marie didn't at first, then she did.

Marie said, "I'm telling you to be careful - same as you were telling me."

Iggy forced a grin and turned away.

He told his wife that a man without control of his mind was a terrifying thing. He wasn't going to let the skull get the best of him. He was alive. He held that thought - only a skull. It couldn't move, nor breathe. He felt a little better now.

"What the hell's that?" Iggy came suddenly alert, his head stretching out on his neck like a wild animal's.

A terrible sound drifted toward them through the attic door - guttural, primitive, ghostly. Marie grabbed his arm but he shook her off and moved out into the hallway. The wind was noisy, hurling rain against the windows. They half ran, half crawled, to the attic door. They reached the attic door where, showing the instincts of a soldier, he slowed and stilled his breath, crouching to look under the door.

Marie was beside him. He slowly opened the door and halted, seeing a shape he did not like, hearing motion, but it was only the wind-battered curtains.

Jumbled images collided in his mind as he groped for

comprehension. Lightning flickered distantly and he saw the skull's glow for the first time. Then again! Another flash of lightning and Marie screamed. Iggy silenced her. The face of the skull was ghastly with glowing crimson eyes. The sight of those glowing sockets drove the strength from him. Unable to move, he stood helpless by the skull.

"It's all right," his voice floated out of the darkness. The next few minutes were hell, walking through the darkness with a glowing skull and one hysterical wife.

It would only take a swing of his arm to wipe out this skull once and for all, he was that close to it, but Marie demanded, "Can't we forget about that skull? I'm tired of all this, I've had enough."

Iggy agreed.

Enough light filtered into the hallway to allow them to see the attic door and make their way back toward their bedroom.

There was nothing to be seen anywhere now. The glowing eyes of the skull were fading to blankness. The wind and rain had stopped.

It had been a long night without sleep, on top of hours of exhausting watch and nervous tension.

Things seemed considerably brighter that morning.

This skull has hounded the family with diabolical energy. A frightening glob on the carpet, clock hands twirling round and round, queer noises, and the skull's power and capacity to move from place to place had added immeasurably to its terror.

Can it be that strength and soul remain in the head after death?

One thing Iggy was very careful to do was to make Marie promise absolutely never to go into the attic alone.

They do not know precisely when the haunting stopped or if it will return again. Until then, they have decided to live with all these strange and bizarre happenings. Now there is nothing to do but go about their daily routine and wait. . . .

Twice a week, when his wife goes shopping and he is alone in the house, Iggy wonders what the prospects are of the glob appearing again; and when he sees the skull at the shelf's edge, he said, that cold feeling becomes colder.

Lock 52, Winter Scene

Sterling Salt Co. canalboat passing by Warren Coal Building

Canalboat leaving double lock 52

R. S. & E. Trolley Stop Shelter - photo by Erna

White's canalboat
(In background, the famous Erie House, built in 1880)

Kern's Gocery Store, north of Lock 52

Guzzo's Racing Car in winner's circle

Masson's Creamery, Conquest, New York

*A special "thank you" to our Historian, Marie VanDetto
for identifying the photos.*

10

The Old Stone House Ghost

The October air was frosty, but the sweat broke out upon Uncle Pete's face as he told me about the frightening experience he had as a young man.

Uncle Pete regularly visited relatives in the next town. It was about a mile's walk from his home, past the site of an apparently haunted stone house.

As the story goes, Farmer Bari was pumping water from the well one warm summer evening and never returned to his family inside the house. His body was found the following night under the pump handle, stuffed in a grain sack. The murder case is unsolved to this day. Some say the old farmer returns every evening to the site of his slaying to haunt the vacant house and perhaps to find his murderer.

It was near midnight when uncle left his relatives and started for home. The road was steep. Every rock he passed, every tree, every foot of the roadway was familiar to him. He kept his eyes turned to the right, sharply scanning every shrub and fence and hiding place in the stone house yard.

When he came opposite the old family burying ground he saw what he had been fearing. A ghostly shadow, half hidden by trees, moved a short distance from him. He dashed on in earnest, trying to seem not to run, managing a sort of gliding half-trot. Suddenly he was struck to shivering terror by a thunderous sound near the roadside, followed by incessant screams of laughter. He began a faster pace, staring only to the ground. For the first, he noticed a bright light shining on his shoes. He wasn't carrying a lantern, as he usually did, and it was a moonless night. There was total darkness, except for his lighted shoes on that lonely road. His hair stood up straight and his legs raced ahead of his body. Puffing, he continued running as fast as he could, but Uncle Pete could not outrun the light.

It was not until he had passed the old well near the stone house and was nearing the next neighbor's fence line that the brilliant light disappeared from his shiny, black shoes. Again there was complete darkness all around him.

Uncle never forgot that night of suspense and terror. It plagued him until his death, last August, at age ninety-two.

11

What is Happening
To Our "John"?

There was a ghost who could not rest because he had been secretly murdered. His knockings on the walls made living in his old house unbearable and the place changed ownership many times. It is a known fact that real estate agents often hush up any tinge of the unusual in a house's history and I suspect they sold many homes in this area, including this one, under similar conditions.

When the person guilty of the crime died, of old age I am told, the rappings stopped.

The present occupants say they had never heard any unusual noises until quite recently, but admit that the old house does rattle and creak a lot when the wind blows across the mucklands.

It was in late autumn when Laurie phoned and said, "This may sound silly but I need to know who first owned this home." I answered that I didn't know but my grandmother bought it in the late nineteenth century. She never lived in it but gave it to her best friend Trizzy as a wedding present.

Laurie then began explaining that something strange was happening to their home.

It began two weeks before her call to me. As she tells it, she and her family were upstairs asleep when the downstairs toilet flushed. She nudged her husband and tried to wake him. Trying to remain calm, she convinced herself that her older daughter must be using it. But upon checking the girls' bedroom, found them both asleep in their beds.

For the rest of the night she tossed and turned, dreading that she would again hear the toilet flush. Yet she decided not to disturb Ken. After all, maybe it was a dream.

She put off closing her eyes until dawn streaked the sky. The incident seemed less frightening in the daylight and she soon forgot about it; that is until Ken's experience a few nights later.

On that particular Sunday evening, the TV programs had many old movies showing and they stayed up very late watching one show after another. They both fell asleep on the sofa.

In the morning Ken complained that he had a terrible night; couldn't sleep because the toilet had "water flowing" sounds coming from it; the toilet flushing kept waking him up. All this happened several times, he remembered. Laurie reminded him of the same noises she had heard earlier in the month. They both complained of a numbness in their arms during these weird bathroom happenings.

"Do you suppose this place is haunted?" she asked.

"Why, have you experienced any other unusual incidents?" I immediately inquired as I reached for my pad and pencil.

She hesitated for awhile then softly whispered, "Well, not to sound foolish, but when Sara was four years old, I heard a loud thump from her room above where she was already in bed. Rushing upstairs I found her sitting up in bed apparently still fast asleep but talking to a vague dark shape that crouched on the floor at the foot of the bed. As I approached, it seemed to disappear into the chimney."

Laurie said she remained level-headed, although she was thoroughly frightened, and asked Sara what that noise was. Had she fallen out of bed? Sara answered no, but her bed was going up and down!

Laurie never told anyone about this scary evening because she knew her friends and relatives would tease her and besides no one would believe it.

But now that her husband is in on this mysterious bathroom thriller, she is telling it all as it happens.

They are both sleeping on the living room sofa again, hoping to catch their invisible guest who needs to use their "John" after midnight.

The River Road Specter

Bill was born in the middle of the deer season in the early years of the depression and was presented with his first BB gun at the age of five. I can still recall his first year with a shotgun. He was fourteen then and with a .20 gauge single shot. He would venture from our home and walk the woods all day long. There was plenty to shoot, the supply of game obviously inexhaustible during that era. He rarely returned from the field empty-handed.

But today hunting is becoming harder and harder for the average sportsman. To find wild game or an open field without the dreaded "POSTED" sign on every fence post, is almost impossible in this area. So when Bill was driving along the River Road and spotted a ring-necked pheasant, he slammed on the brakes of his old pick-up truck, floored the pedal and made a one-eighty degree turn into the farm's driveway. He quickly jumped out and knocked on the farmhouse door.

An elderly lady answered the loud knocking and Bill asked permission to hunt on her property. He told her about the pheasant. She said yes and as he turned to leave he heard her coughing. He glanced back and saw that she was leaning over the kitchen sink, choking. He rushed inside and immediately began to help her. His training with the medics during World War II quickly came back to him and he knew how to handle this emergency. After she coughed up the piece of meat that was lodged in her throat, she felt a bit shaky and grabbed Bill's hand for support. He found her hand uncommonly cold which made him eye the old woman more closely. Whereupon, he observed that in speaking she never moved her lips, nor her eyes.

She thanked him for being so kind, waved a hand and mysteriously disappeared. He thought can this be a normal lady? Her body was solid but she was icy cold.

He drove immediately to the Central Hotel. He needed a strong drink to calm him down. Saving an old woman's life wasn't something one does every day.

At the bar, Bill told the few customers who patronized the bar daily about his hunting experience on the nearby farm. How he saved the owner's life. His story had a happy ending, as always, for he shot the pheasant on his way out of the driveway. All in a day's work, he bragged.

They all listened and laughed a little uneasily. When he had finished his much too long tale, they patted him on the shoulder and said, "Bill, that old woman has been dead over ten years! She choked to death on a piece of meat!"

Bill picked comedy as he met it and passed it on to others. But not today, this was not the time or place.

He closed his big, blue eyes and began to recite the old English-Irish prayer his wife had taught him:

From Bogles and bugaboos,
Warlocks and Ghosties,
And things that go wump in the night,
Good Lord, deliver ME!

The next few days had the quality of a nightmare. Fear in a fearful situation is normal. But this was frightening to him and to his family. Did he see a ghost? Was he acting rationally? Not long afterward there were stories that people had noticed a mysterious old lady night and day about the farm. The figure always disappeared before their eyes.

These stories were treated with respect after the experience of Bill, who recounted his "life-saving" ordeal with the choking woman as often as he found listeners.

There are many tales of horses and dogs behaving as though they had seen or sensed something invisible to their human companions as they travel along the River Road.

Neighbors say that the old one was a much loved woman with a large circle of acquaintances. She always told them she would meet them after death on her farm. When she died many years later, her loyal friends accompanied her to the grave site. She has never appeared to any of them.

Not long ago Bill paid a return visit to the farm and had a long talk with the present owner. She told him she sees the old woman's specter sometimes late at night walking in and out of rooms. During the daylight hours, the specter's footsteps, heavy and ponderous, seem to pass her along the corridor although she sees nothing.

Just when you think "she" has moved out of the farmhouse, she reappears.

Her dog always showed every sign of being terrified during this period, growling and snarling at no visible presence, and often trying to scratch and dig its way under the furniture.

One evening the dog couldn't be made to stay in its doghouse. As the dog began to run back up the house steps, it suddenly stopped dead in its tracks. They found the animal whimpering and shivering and looking up the stairs. When they glanced in that direction, they saw a ghostly figure on the porch landing, coming down toward them. When the figure reached the first step, it turned and slowly moved across the lawn to vanish in the gloom.

Almost hidden and forgotten, this farmhouse is still haunted regularly by this unhappy specter who is said to be doomed to remain earthbound forever because she seems to be searching for something or someone.

Billy believes in ghosts for the best of reasons - he has seen one!

13

Marie could remember every single detail of that curious night just as clearly as if it were yesterday.

She could switch it on in her memory anytime she liked and run it through in front of her eyes exactly as though it were the reel of a cinema film, and it never varied.

Marie said, "I am going to try to write it down quite simply, just as it happened. I shall try not to exaggerate anything."

From Marie's handwritten story:

Many years ago when I was a teenager, my mother, sister and I went downtown - at the time we always spoke of it as "going to the village." It was a Saturday night. It was warm. The sky was beautiful and all was quiet.

We did some shopping then stopped at Power's Ice Cream Parlor, located near the Trolley Station on Main Street for refreshments.

We walked slowly and took a shorter route home, via the Towpath. We could walk that way now as the canal was closed. The Erie closed in 1916.

I should mention here that we had a very dear friend and neighbor who lived near the Towpath. Her front door faced the Towpath and her back door faced Maiden Lane.

Her name was Kate Rancier. I loved Kate very much. She had an old organ and she would always ask me to play some favorite hymn for her.

Kate died suddenly and all of us in our house missed her very much. She was our adopted grandmother.

I always remember Kate's beautiful rose bush by her front door. The roses were single roses, very light pink in colour. When she was alive, she always brought my mother a large bouquet.

It so happened that we went downtown, as usual, for several years after Kate passed away and always on Saturday night. That seemed to be the custom in our town.

On this particular night, I said aloud, "I have had this strong feeling when passing the Rancier home at night and even in the brilliant sunlight of day, that someone is waiting for me." My mother teased with the reply, "A new beau, perhaps?" I quickly changed the subject. We were all in such a happy mood, why ruin it with all these eerie thoughts.

As we came to Kate's house, something moved in the shadows of the rose bush. My heart shot up into my throat. Mother caught hold of my little sister, trembling like a leaf.

We said to each other, "Did you see THAT?" We all agreed that we saw a tall lady dressed in a cloudy white dress. Her dark hair was piled high on her head in a topknot. She stood by that lovely pink rose bush smiling and looking very human.

Startled by the sudden and inexplicable appearance, we stopped in our tracks.

At first we didn't know what to do.

"Did you see that woman?" Mother asked. Her voice rose higher than normal and I knew she was a little frightened.

The figure in white began to move around the pink blossoms. As it silently walked toward us, its hand was moving so slowly that it did not seem to move at all.

In my mind I told myself, "This is Kate; and I am not afraid."

With a valiant effort I succeeded at last in stretching out my hand towards the apparition. Suddenly it turned around as if to listen. We knew at once that the face was that of Kate. It had a strange, mournful beauty to it.

As I continued to gaze at the spectral image, I saw her eyes looking at me. One moment I seemed to distinguish them clearly, the next they seemed gone. But still two rays of a pale blue light frequently shot through the darkness.

After staring at us for a moment, the figure placed her ghostly white hand upon a rose, whereupon its delicate petals floated gently to the ground. She seemed to be trying to catch them, but almost as soon as she was aware of my extended hand, she strolled clear of the rose bush and, without looking either way, silently passed by and disappeared back of the house.

We were genuinely puzzled, amazed and decided to see who it was. We could find no trace of her anywhere, nor indeed of anyone. We waited a short time, shivering and afraid to talk.

A feeling of intense cold seized me. One moment before she had been there and we had heard no sound. It took some time for the truth to register. We saw what might be called, indeed must be called, for there is no other description - the spirit of Kate dressed in white!

Just then we had neither the wish or strength to rationalize this haunting experience. It was all we could do to get our feet going towards home.

It has served as a perennial topic of conversation, of course, but the whole of that evening's experience was one that I would never have voluntarily undergone again.

"I always think of Kate as I drive by her old house on Maiden Lane and Towpath Road," Marie remarked as we walked along the bank of the old Erie.

Marie realized, with genuine uneasiness, that we were now walking down the very path where this peculiar incident had taken place over seventy years ago.

At that moment I wished I was miles from the spot because there was not a rose bush in sight, yet the sweet fragrance of roses mysteriously drifted by us.

Was that Kate welcoming her dear friend Marie?